Text copyright © 2015 by Corinne Fenton
Illustrations copyright © 2015 by Andrew McLean

First U.S. edition 2016

Library of Congress Catalog Card Number 2015941709
ISBN 978-0-7636-8097-8

APS 21 20 19 18 17 16
10 9 8 7 6 5 4 3 2 1

Printed in Humen, Dongguan, China

MIX
Paper from responsible sources
FSC® C101537
www.fsc.org

This book was typeset in Goudy Old Style.
The illustrations were done in watercolor, charcoal, and pencil.

Candlewick Press
99 Dover Street
Somerville, Massachusetts 02144

visit us at www.candlewick.com

*For Sugar and Cinnamon, waiting where
they wandered under the wattle and gums.*

C. F.

*For all our wonderful dogs.
You can measure your life in dogs.*

A. M.

Special thanks to Ron Fluck OAM for his expert
advice and wisdom, and to Maryann Ballantyne
for believing we could do it.

Bob the Railway Dog

The True Story of an Adventurous Dog

CORINNE FENTON   *illustrated by* ANDREW McLEAN

CANDLEWICK PRESS

In those hushed moments before sunset, a train crept, hissing and sighing, into Carrieton Station, South Australia. It was September 1884.

Running the train that night were a driver, a fireman, and a guard—Will Ferry.

Among the cargo was a motley lot of homeless dogs that had come up from Adelaide.

They were on their way to be rabbit hunters in outback South Australia.

When Guard Ferry spied one of the pups smiling at him, it was as if they'd met before.

"Well, what do we have here?" Ferry said as he ruffled the pup's fur.
The pup looked up at Guard Ferry, and something tumbled in the man's heart.

When the rest of the dogs went on their way, there was one that stayed behind.

Guard Ferry named him Bob.

Every day Bob trotted to the station with his master,
and every evening he was there, waiting, when the train returned.
One morning, as the train was inching away from the station,
Guard Ferry looked back at Bob.
"Come on, then, fella," he said. And faster than a lightning flash,
Bob jumped up into the caboose.

From that day on, Bob traveled
regularly with Guard Ferry on
the wheat special train
all the way up to Quorn.

In those early days of the railway, shiny new tracks like spiderwebs were opening up vast areas of Australia. Trains were the link from mining town to farming town. Trains arrived with supplies and left with the town's produce. Wheat, cattle, sheep, and of course passengers traveled by train.

Bob would jump into
the cab of one train,

leap off at some wayside spot, then clamber onto
a train heading in the opposite direction.

There was hardly a town in South Australia he did not visit, from Oodnadatta to Kalangadoo.

His favorite spot was on a Yankee engine or on the
coal tender with the whistle echoing and wild smoke
billowing around him. He stood there when the night train ran,
only the glow of one lonely beam unstitching the black-opal
night, while spinifex bushes peeped from beside the tracks
like woolly-headed ghosts.

When the Adelaide-to-Melbourne Intercolonial Railway opened in 1887,
Bob could travel even farther. There was hustle and bustle and a
flurry of farewells at the busy stations, and Bob was part of it all.

He was welcome in any porter's room at any station. Everyone knew Bob the Railway Dog.
At the end of each day he would follow a driver or guard home for the night.

Wherever there were train tracks, or tracks being laid,
Bob was there. If a train was heading to an important event,
Bob was sure to be on it.

It is said Bob was a distinguished guest at the Melbourne Centennial
International Exhibition and at the opening of the Hawkesbury
River Railway Bridge in New South Wales. Some say he was even
spotted up north in Queensland.

Every so often, Bob called in to visit his old friend, Guard Ferry. But Bob was a wanderer.
The moment a train chugged and chuffed and the whistle blew, Bob jumped aboard.

Bob had adventure in his heart and the
rattle of the rails in his soul. He was
everyone's friend, Bob the Railway Dog.

Author's Note

Bob was a regular visitor to Adelaide Station, where his photo still sits
behind a framed glass window. And at the National Railway Museum
in Port Adelaide you can see Bob's special collar, a gift from
the railway men he loved, engraved with the words
"Stop me not but let me jog, for I am Bob the driver's dog."